AF654290

SandDunes

Rinzen

Aswin Subhan

Assistant Engineer
(Irrigation Department, Kerala State)
Other interests: Digital Art,
Voice Artist, Story Writing, Lyric Writer.
Education: Btech, Mtech

Hometown : Thripunithura, Ernakulam.

Email: aswinsubhan@gmail.com

Novel

Rinzen

Aswin Subhan

SandDunes

SandDunes
an imprint of green books private limited
gb building, civil lane road, ayyanthole,
thrissur- 680 003, kerala
ph: +91 487-2381066, 2381039
website: www.greenbooksindia.com
e-mail: info@greenbooksindia.com

branches:
thrissur 8589095302
thiruvananthapuram 8589095301
calicut 8589095307

english
rinzen
novel
by
aswin subhan

published december 2024

cover design : aswathi d meppilly

printed in india

isbn : 978-93-48125-55-2

₹ 150.00
SDGBPL/14/2024

Prelude

Zen shed light to live life with clarity, love and consciousness rather than creating scars with stuffed philosophies. "It's not like spirituality should be a part of you, instead you should become a part of spirituality" – when I read that line in this book, a light from the horizon spreads all through my being, and that is what Zen means.

We all have heard a lot about Mulla Nasruddin and his funny stories. Usually, we include him in comic literature, as we see him cracking jokes and sometimes making himself a laughing stock. Actually, we all realised the master in him through the discourses of mystics like Osho. When we read in this book, the way how the Zen master Bankei narrates the stories of Mulla Nasruddin to his disciple Rinzen, suddenly we feel like laughing at ourselves.

When, Mulla Nasruddin answers the question "why searching here if you know you lost it there" as "I can't search it where I lost it, since it's so dark there- but here there is light!" -it appears to be funny in prima facie, and we laugh at it. But when we penetrate to the inner meaning, laughter paves way to thinking- which brings a question – "aren't we all doing the same? Searching for ourselves in wrong places?"

Merging Zen and Sufism, how beautifully this small novel unravels the hidden reality of life's unbridled freedom.

Simple, pure, elegant and soothing.

Like the breeze, like the river, like the meadows.

When I completed reading, a fresh smile blossomed on my face, and an inner voice murmured: "Life is not in fullness, but in emptiness"

Dear Aswin Subhan, keep writing like this, for it shall be light unto people, that all their burdens may be light.

with love,

Shaukkath

RINZEN

Intentions

Unhurriedly, the horse drawn carriage moved through the snowy forest path. Tall oak trees stood like guards on either side of the road, shading the entire area. It was evening. Comfortably, Rinzen sat inside the cart, goggling the majestic scenery through the small window. Four horses pulled that cart-two of them were caramel coloured and two were black. The coachman didn't seem worried at all, although the snow layers were more than a half-foot thick. "It's a severe winter this month" Rinzen said to herself. The cart was well built. Not even a bit of cold air came inside. The finely detailed Zitan wood cabin smelled of patchouli oil.

"This place looks so deserted" Rinzen asked. "Don't worry madam. This route is frequently taken by Knights and archers of the emperor while they do their surveillance rounds. Thieves cannot be in here. And moreover, you have hired the best Coachman."

That sounded a bit overconfident to Rin. Being tired from a long journey and not ready to start a long conversation, Rin simply nodded, smiled and asked-

"So, I can sleep peacefully, until we reach Fushun?"

"Of course." An all-confident coachman replied.

Rinzen tried to find a place to settle to sleep. It was then she had a clear look at how the inside of the cart was- sacks, jars, linen rolls, sealed wooden boxes, ceramics and smelly packages sealed with wood resin- must be dried sea fish, stacked in there like books in a thick library, leaving barely a seating space for her. Sometimes people cannot see even with their eyes open, for their eyes are lost to the mind inside -Rinzen too. She was in a hurry when she booked the ride.

"What are all these!"

"It's business. A side hustle. I sell them at rural markets like Fushun-anything can get more price there"

Anger had started to breach Rin's throat.

"It's almost like... you have brought an entire grocery shop with you!! Well, whatever....but there is no space to sleep!" that was a statement as well as a question.

"You can sit and sleep" coachman replied instantly- and there was not even a hint of apology in his tone.

"How can someone 'sit' and sleep?"

"Haven't you seen those statues of Buddha? He used to sleep like that"

"Buddha was meditating, you fool." Rinzen gulped the last part of her words.

She lifted her bags from her lap, kept them beside the coachman's luggage- every person in the world has their luggage. She was angry to the nose level but there was nothing she could do. Rinzen had learnt how to keep quiet in such situations. Almost 10 years ago- when she was about 18 years old, and studying in a Buddhist monastery in Lhasa- one day her master told her about the dangers of sudden anger. He said -"Take a ball of steel to the river. It will instantly sink in water; but if you press it, make it into a foil, and fold it to the shape of a vessel, it floats!! It's a lesson to learn, Rin; the steel ball, when transformed to the right shape, becomes a friend of water. The water will support it. In the same manner, we humans should transform ourselves according to the situations we are in. Only then we will be able to enjoy the good side of every circumstance we come across."

Rinzen closed her eyes, took a deep breath, exhaled out all that anger. After a while of pushing and pulling, somehow, she found a sleeping position amidst those luggage blocks. A wisdom quote she read from a book came to her mind- she read that a few years ago, at some library. It had a chapter about the things humans should learn from animals. And from dogs, it was sleep. Humans should learn how to sleep like stray dogs- for they are satisfied with whichever place they got to sleep. If a sleeping dog is driven away from its place, it will simply go and lie down at another spot, and continue the sleep as if nothing happened. No protests, no complaints, no anger- they are contented. But humans- even inside the most luxurious bedrooms, they are sleepless. Luxury is often a lame representations of actual needs.

Facing the roof, Rinzen laid on her back, and stretched her arms until she heard some knuckles cracking. The linen rolls made a comfortable pillow for her overwrought and tired head. She could see the beautiful silhouettes of those oak tree tops through the window. She couldn't interpret whether they were a lucid dream or reality. When every part of the body falls asleep, but the eyes are half-awake, whatever that is seen would feel like a dream. She felt like she sank into the floor. Her eyes started to feel weighted. Lucid visuals faded. Slowly, she entered a deep sleep.

The wooden cart darted through the forest. Sunlight had completely vanished. It was twilight-the pathway became darker, windy and foggy. White snow became bluish. There were 3 lamps- one was a candle lamp which was inside the cart, and two were oil filled glass clad brass lamps fitted near the coachman's seat, in-front of the carriage. It barely lit the road ahead.

"OYYY....""" A loud call from outside. Rin woke up, as her cart stopped suddenly. She looked outside to see three men standing in-front of a broken cart, in the middle of the road. The wind was freezing cold.

"We are trapped in here. Can you help us reach the next town? See, you can use our horses."

Two big black majestic horses were tied to that carriage. The wooden cart looked opulent. There was not even an inch of space on the outer body of that Huanghuali wood cart left without an artistic carving job. The cart, the horses, the three men- everything looked posh.

Rinzen looked at her coachman.

"Sorry, we don't have enough space..." Coachman frowned.

"Please, at least give us a helping hand. We can together work to take this wheel out of the snow" one of the three men requested.

"We are merchants." he added.

"Let us help them." Rin said.

She knew the dangers of the forest- bears, tigers, or wolves or an unnamed animal from the folklore-anything can come for a hunt in the midnight. Habitually, when a danger is sensed, Rin anticipates the worst-case scenarios.

"They might get frostbite" Covering up her fear, an anxious Rinzen said to the coachman.

Reluctantly, he joined.

Rinzen and the coachman placed their hands on the sunken wheel. Two of the merchants pushed the cart from back. One of them sat at the front and took reins of the horses.

None of them were Kung fu masters- the five of them combined could only tilt the cart a little. After a quarter hour of backbreaking, apart from the night getting colder and their hands getting sweatier, nothing changed- the cart didn't move an inch.

"It's the snow. We will need a heavier push." Coachman enlightened.

The merchants seemed hopeless. Rinzen had no answer.

Coachman looked around, and listened to the surroundings for a few seconds, then stated: "Untie your horses. Let them rest under the trees. There must be a stream nearby- I can hear it; and there must be enough grass near it... If you want fire sticks and some food, I can give you that" he told the merchants, showing a hand gesture for money.

Hopelessly, one of the merchants stepped forward and gave some coins.

While Rinzen was thinking of ways to help the three men, Coachman was making arrangements for them to stay in the forest. He gave them firewood, dried fish, cooking oil, a pot.

Handing them a sack of lentils, he said "Feed this to those horses- tomorrow, they will dart like an arrow. This is the best feed you can get anywhere".

Rinzen could only sit and watch her coachman's rapid business growth.

After telling them how to get near the stream, and to wait until he came back in the morning, he returned to the cart and took the rein.

"Let's get going, it's dark"

Coachman's voice sounded a bit commanding. Perplexed and gloomy, a half-minded Rinzen steps inside the cart, but suddenly noticed something and stopped. She exclaimed:

"Salt!"

Coachman turned his head: "Yea, what about it?"

Rinzen didn't answer. She shouted out loud, to the merchants who were untying their horses already. "Stop! I will get you out of here."

Rin bit on and opened a salt sack from the luggage, hurried to the merchant's cart, spilled it around the sunken wheel.

"Now see."

The curious three men pushed that cart wheel, and it slid like as if it stood on butter.

"Whooooah!!! Great!!!" the Merchants celebrated.

Rin didn't forget to make the merchants pay to the coachman for the salt bags- she is very particular with the value of things.

Rinzen got inside her cart. "Now let us get going".

An hour of journey passed. It was nearly midnight. The gallop of horses wasn't enough to pierce the deep silence of the forest. It was majestically quiet.

"That was great, Madam." Said the coachman.

"What?" an indifferent Rinzen calmly asked.

"Your intelligence"

Rinzen: "That's common knowledge. People use salt to melt ice"

Coachman: "Yes. I also knew it, I have seen it, but I wasn't able to think of such a solution at the time. I just couldn't connect it. That's what I meant. you are very intelligent"

Rinzen: "You too are. Everyone is intelligent in some way. It's only that, intelligence grows where your interest is. You were not at all interested in helping those people. You were thinking about picking them up on your way back; so that you could charge them a good fare! Your intelligence was working on profit. You had the intellect to figure out there was a stream nearby, by just listening to the subtle sounds. And you realized and suggested that it could be a resting spot for them. That was a sharp intelligence. See, it's all about the intentions one has!!"

Coachman sighed. A few minutes of silence passed.

"Where do you want to go in Fushun?"

"I am going to Bankei's temple. To study there"

Coachman exclaimed: "Oh, the story teller monk"

"What?" Rinzen got curious. "Have you heard of him? How?"

Rinzen did not expect the coachman to have knowledge about Zen masters.

"I have heard that he tells stories to the people who seek advice from him. I heard from the shopkeepers in the market. I am quite familiar with the people there."

He continued:

"Being a coachman, I have met almost every kind of person; sometimes monks come for a ride in my cart; sometimes fishermen; sometimes professors; sometimes thieves. And I am telling, you talk like a wise person- and you are well educated it seems to me- and skilled too! Then why do you want to study more? That too at a temple?" The coachman had his visions about life.

Rinzen said: "I have a room full of resources, but it seems I've lost the key"

The horse drawn carriage moved slowly.

Temple

Next morning, the cart stoped in-front of a big gate, right below a snowy hill. Sun had started to shine over the hills already, but the dense tree tops let only a little sunlight to touch the ground. The woods looked like as if they didn't want the night to end. Forests love darkness.

Rinzen, who was sound asleep, woke up to hearing her coachman say out loud - "This is the place, Madam".

Rinzen paid him very well. After passing good wishes, the coachman and his cart left. The rock pillared metal gate was open. Behind the gate, there was a beige stone clad stepped pathway, going all the way up to the hill top. Rinzen rushed to the gates of the temple.

"This is the place where I will find my path to Nirvana" Rinzen told herself, as she climbed the steps of that Zen temple, atop beautiful mountains of Northern Zhongguo*. Thoughts accelerated her legs. Intermixed spots of sunlight and shades of tree canopies laid out fascinating patterns on the ground- resembling a kaleidoscope. Rinzen used to make

---

* *ancient name of China*

kaleidoscopes when she was a kid. She liked their beauty. They made an attractive sight, irrespective of how the coloured glass bits are aligned- a pattern in clutter- an order in chaos- kaleidoscopes were always an insightful experience to Rinzen. In less than half an hour she reached the hill top. There was a fenced courtyard. A beautifully kept round garden, encircled by the nicely worked stone building of the temple, shingled roofs, timber pillars. All the main walls were clad by wood, incense burning smell everywhere. Monks, wearing brown Zhiduo walked peacefully in the garden. Some stout men, seemed like security guards walked vigilantly, holding bamboo sticks.

"New student?" a voice from the back. Rinzen turned suddenly, and there was a bald headed, serious looking monk looking at her.

Rin suddenly corrected her voice and posture.

"Yes sir"

"Name?"

"Rinzen"

The Monk called in a security guard. Rinzen was taken to a room.

She sat opposite to the monk- and between them a large stone table was there. The only thing warm inside that room was the candle burning on the table top. The security guard opened and took a look at the things inside her bags. Most of them were books.

The Monk calmly watched as the guard took out and placed the books one by one on the table. After emptying the book-bag, the guard opened the other one- and it had clothes, paper rolls, quill pen and ink.

"Are you a scholar? Why so many science texts" The monk asked.

Rinzen: "Those are from my previous schools. I like math, science and philosophy. I used to participate in contests too. That's why"

Monk waved his hand to the security man, ordering him to re-pack the bag. Guard obeyed without delay.

The Monk and the guard had cold faces. They almost looked as if they were carved out of rock. Rinzen placed her hands on the table. The granite stone counter felt ice cold.

"Mm-hm… so… what if I say that numbers exist only in our imagination, and the reality is only physical science?" an unexpected question from the Monk.

"That's what Plato said about numbers- they are abstract entities."

"I want to know your views about the matter-not what you read about it"

"Okay- I agree on that. Mathematics is imaginary" Rinzen, since a liker of debates, politely answered without any hesitation.

She added, "But it works"

"Can you elaborate"

"For example, you have 3 carrots. Your mind will know you have one carrot when you see one. And when you see the next one, you have a memory of the last one. And for the third one, you have the memory of past two. This is what counting is. It's a mental image of repetition of a certain kind of unit. But your memory cannot process big quantities. Say it's a thousand carrots. You cannot remember and mentally process one by one- So you need math. We have symbols and numbers to represent operations and quantities."

"Good. What is the meaning of number 'zero'" The monk calmly asked his next one.

"Zero is the base of all counts."

The monk took a deep breath, passing a shrewd look.

"Do you think the number zero bears a significance in the realm of spirituality- from a philosopher's point of vision?"

Rinzen: "Everything, every concept and every matter that appears in the physical world can have a philosophical meaning too- that's what I think."

"Go on" the indifferent monk said.

"Yes. From what I have understood, zero can represent the state of an extremely clear mind -where there are no thoughts. Almost thirty to thirtyfive thoughts come to an average human mind every minute. Zero state is when you go back to the base-withdrawing from everything. Where there are no compulsions. No thoughts-no affecting memories. And that deep state is so dominant, that it would not allow anymore thoughts to come up. Like the mathematical operation- anything when multiplied to zero, becomes zero again."

"Well, what if you 'add' "

"Thoughts don't 'add'. They multiply. One thought gives birth to two or three other thoughts, and each one of them brings two -three new thoughts- that's how it progresses; like a tree spreading its branches"

"I will let you choose a geometrical shape. Circle, triangle, rectangle. Which one you think is special? And why?"

"Every shape has its significance"

"Mm-hm. That's a broader view. But I want you to answer the question?"

Rinzen took a pause. She remembered as much knowledge as she could- which she gained from her previous schools.

"Triangle is a three-point figure. In this world, all living beings are thought of or remembered in one of its three forms only. As a foetus, a walking body, and as a memory after its death. Nobody thinks of a person before his birth! Also, time is referred to as past, present and future. Three stages!"

"That's enough" Monk smiled. He slowly stood up, and bowed to Rinzen as a welcoming gesture.

"You can join classes tomorrow."

It was then Rinzen realized that it was a test.

Rinzen walked behind the guard, through the corridor. Incense smell had started to subside. Their footsteps made mild thuds on the bamboo floor. At the end of the corridor, the guard stopped in-front of a large burgundy wooden door. That 7 feet high door had all the markings a hostel door could ever have; nail marks, random 'artworks', burned spots-might be from incense sticks; or from tobacco rolls smoked by earlier inmates…the metallic lock plate looked a bit rusted. The guard took out a long key from his pocket and opened the door. He left the key with Rin.

A stone table, a wooden shelf, a cotton filled cot. Everything was kept in place neatly, as it should be. Zen temples are always like that. Order and orientation are of utmost importance. Unused things will be thrown away in no time. Just like the mind of an enlightened Zen monk, her room was clear off all unnecessary things. "So…my mind is the only thing in this room which has needless things in it" Rinzen self- mocked.

Rinzen decided to take a bath. There was hot water in the tub, to which before she entered, rinsed her hair thoroughly with rice water, which was kept in a bucket, and there was a bowl beside. The bath powder was ground white bean and clove, the fragrance of which had a luxurious appeal.

Rinzen thought of a story. Somebody asked Buddha "What is gained when you become enlightened? "Buddha said "Nothing is gained. When I became enlightened, I just came to know that I lost a lot of things. Anger, sadness, compulsiveness, grief, anxiety and so on."

Next Day

Rinzen sat on lotus pose for a while. Closing her eyes, she took a deep breath. The breath washed all her thoughts into her heart. There were certain things that Rinzen practised- remnants from her past life- the incomplete quests she made to quench her thirst for freedom. She then gently made an affirmation, to her heart: "Be in harmony with me... Be kind to me, and I shall calmly swim across all of you"- the mantra was made by Rin herself. While chanting, she would take its meaning to her heart, concentrating on it, blending with it. Rinzen was excited about the class. She had heard a lot of this temple, and the Master Bankei. There must be a lot of notes to take down, she thought. Rinzen had a cache of writing paper, made from boiled mulberry bark pulp which she used for her notes and diary; and a few rolls of expensive high- quality paper, made of seaweed and sandalwood bark- which she sourced from a friend who worked at a printing house. His name was Guo, a classmate from her philosophy school. His job was to help cut the paper to required size and to ink the letter-carved wooden cubes onto which the paper would be pressed. The strict owner of that press never allowed blemished or torn paper sheets to go into printing, which helped Guo to find a lot of such unused, slightly damaged paper sheets. He used to sell them at a quarter of its original price, but to Rinzen, he gave them free. "Dear Rin, this is imperial paper- and has no damage at all, I checked. Only use it for a special occasion. Take it Rin, for I am thankful to you in many ways, without you I would have never passed those tests. And I am sure you are going to become a great person one day."

Rinzen took out 3-4 sheets of her imperial paper, a quill pen and ink, and headed to the master. "There will be a lot to learn, I must take down all his words" she said to herself.

The morning looked so pure and warm. She could hear the loud and high pitched "Haa" "Woooh" "Yuooo"– howls from the Kung fu students, doing their morning drill in the side-yard. Monks and students on duty were seen cleaning the blackened oil lamps hung on pillars.

She walked to the next building, across the garden. Warm sunlight was busy planting diamonds on the red roof shingles. In a short time, she reached the doorstep of the meditation hall.

Master Bankei was seen gently sitting on the floor, on a cloth. Upon seeing Rin at the door, he waved his hands to let her in. She sat on the floor, infront of him. Rinzen saw that the Master's hand movements had a meditative attire.

When Master seemed like he was about to say something, Rin took out her notebook. She placed the ink bottle beside her, dipped the quill pen, and sharpened her eyes and ears.

A few monks were sitting at the far corners of the hall, meditating. Apart from Rinzen, there were no other students. Master Bankei greeted Rinzen with a pleasant smile, and suddenly closed his eyes for a few minutes. That silence had a thousand verses. Opening his eyes, master came back from the wordless speech. Suddenly, he started telling a story.

One day, Mullah Nasruddin was seen walking around the street lamp near his house, looking down at the ground, searching for something. It was already midnight. His wife came out of the house and asked him, "What are you searching? Did you lose something?" "Yes, I've lost my key," said Nasruddin. "Oh, I see. Don't worry. I will help you find it," said the wife. An hour passed, and his wife was exhausted. "Do you remember just where exactly you might have dropped it?" she asked. "Yes. I dropped it somewhere in the basement of our house," Nasruddin answered. "Then why the hell are you looking for it out here? Don't you know that it is of no use searching it in here?" she shouted in anger. "It's dark in the basement, but here there is more light" Nasruddin said.

"Meditate on the story; come back with your explanation of it. That's the lesson for today." Bankei slowly stood up.

He bowed to Rin, and left.

The empty papers smiled at Rinzen.

Holes

That evening, Master Bankei was seen ambling in the flower garden, watering plants. As usual, he wore a blissful look in his eyes. There was not even a hint of an unwanted movement in his kinesics. As pleasant as possible he walked, as quiet as possible his footsteps were. To those flowers, he was a cool pampering mountain breeze.

Rinzen, after a short nap, came out of her room. She walked through the agarwood incense smoke filled veranda, thinking about an explanation to the story. Flowers in the garden looked pleasant. Peaceful gardeners watered them. Contented Zen monks.

Rinzen is a subtle thinker. She would take a walk, or watch the sunset, or even have a tea and listen to the birds chirping whenever she wanted to find answers to difficult questions; letting the mind work in the backdrop, precisely- her way of thinking.

After a round along the veranda, Rinzen stepped down to the garden. With every step, the water from the wet green grass kept breaching her linen sandals, leaving a churning sound. Scrupulously walking along the less wetted spots, she gazed at the flower plants, like a kid amidst the Huazhao festival parade. She remembered going to that festival when she was little, all those flower-clad boats and beautiful women adorned with floral trinkets.

Every flower had something to symbolize. Lily indicates harmony and unity, Hibiscus is symbol of prosperity, Peony- the king of flowers meant wealth, honour and royalty, and orchids represent nobility and integrity. But Rinzen admired flowers in a bit different way. Her favourite one was Lotus, since it had a satisfying geometrical symmetry to it- always she used to wonder how perfectly those petals are arranged. And then came Hibiscus- not at all symmetric, but what she liked about it was that it came in a large variety of colours- red, pink, white and even blue! “If I were the one to name flowers, I would have called it ‘elephant-ear’ ” Rinzen used to think so, since Hibiscus petals reminded her of an elephant’s ears. Orchids had a special place for her due to their ability to grow on rocks and tree barks- unlike those soil rooted plants. If there is a will to grow, there is a way to grow- that’s what orchids are. They are admirable.

There were a few monks working in the garden - watering, nurturing, mowing- everyone did different jobs; but the one thing common among them was the serene contented smile they all had. She wondered how they looked up to her and smiled just at the right moment when she got near them. Rinzen felt that the nature around was connected to those monks in some manner-otherwise how could one know someone is behind, without looking? They all looked so genuinely blended up with the garden- like apples in an apple tree. She remembered a tantric wisdom- “One who does something with extreme level of affection and concentration, becomes a part of it, and gets reborn”

Every person in the temple had to offer a service. Some people had to work in the kitchen, some in the cleaning department, and some in the garden. A Zen temple is not for lazy people.

Twilight fell in the courtyard. Oil lamps kindled. Sky as well as the mountains wore the same shade- deep blue; the colour of silence. Rinzen took few more rounds in the garden. Cold valley breeze swept past her.

At the centre of the garden, there stood the master-just like any other monk working there. A hungry person’s eyes would see only food- Rinzen’s eyes saw only enlightenment- she saw the calmness- the people who have meditative mind, stands different in any crowd- without wearing anything different or doing anything different- but they are but the most indifferent; unaffected. Master Bankei wore a brown coloured long loose gown, which covered all his feet- and yet it didn’t touch the ground. He held a sprinkling can in his hand- with which he lovingly gave water to those beautiful lily plants. Rinzen walked up to him.

“Rin, what made you come to my temple? “

Bankei asked in his gentle voice.

Although Rin understood the master sensed her presence, she didn’t expect a question there.

"I am in search of Nirvana. I want to become an enlightened one." Rinzen opened up straight without being timid.

"You already are one" Master replied, while continuing the watering job. The lily plants didn't seem any different.

Rinzen said: "That is a sentence said by every Zen master I have met so far."

Some of the monks, hearing that, turned their heads and looked at her with raised eyebrows. They have never heard someone talk to the Master like that.

Master smiled.

"Interesting. How many masters you have come across?"

Rin: "I studied math, philosophy, science- and a lot of other things. But I couldn't complete any of the courses. My mind never allowed me to stay at any place for long. Even though I gained a lot of knowledge, my mind constantly asked for deeper answers-and now I stand here, with nothing. I wandered for ten years; three years before, I started my spiritual journey. I have met eight Zen masters. I have been searching for the truth. Unfortunately, no temple gave me what I wanted"

"What was your experience."

"Well, I did whatever job they assigned to me, meditated for hours and hours. learned sacred teachings; practiced mantras; I concentrated on it like there was nothing else left in me; everything they taught me, I did it. Improving my mind's concentration was the only thing I did -for long three years of my life. But I am still confused."

Master looked at her.

"You didn't get it from those eight temples and still, you think you are going to get it from here? This is just another Zen temple. And I have nothing new to offer you, kid"

"Even a cat has nine lives. Let me try my ninth and last temple, Master."

Bankei passed a blissful smile, and took a sickle out from his scarf and handed it to Rin.

"Clear off the weeds" he said.

Rinzen nodded. She grabbed the beechwood handled sickle.

"Be careful with that" Bankei told as he left. Most of the monks and on-duty students left the garden following the master. It was past twilight, and the air had turned foggy, the only persons still in the courtyard were Rinzen and a few guards.

She swung the sickle in air to check her grip. It was a little bit too heavy for her hands; it kept on slipping away from her hold. Although she had learnt yogic poses, she felt her mind-body coordination was not enough to wield a weapon, for her hands were best suited for pen and paper. Heedfully, she started off from one end of the yard. Snatching the heads of grass, swinging the sickle right at the root level. The sickle was sharp like a Katana, so she didn't have to swing it too wide as she expected- which solved the slipping problem. After a few more swings she became adept in it. But what confused her was that it was so hard to differentiate weeds from flower plants, and flower plants from weeds. Standing near each section of the garden, she had to carefully examine each plant, identify it and act accordingly. Weeds grow when the owner neglects the garden. Unguarded they grow; along with the flowers. They eat the same soil, take the same daylight, nourish from the same water; yet they make the garden go barbarous, unlike the flower plants.

Hours passed. Rinzen almost finished her job. A big heap of garbage looked at her with a grim face, at the corner of the yard.

“Impressive. You really are a hard-worker it seems.” Master Bankei suddenly appeared beside her.

Rinzen nodded. She wiped off the sweat from her forehead.

“Rin, how are you going to dispose off this garbage?” Bankei asked.

“I have dug a pit to bury it, master”

“Well, now where are you going to bury all that soil you dug out to make the pit? “

Rinzen’s grip loosened. Her thoughts came to an end. A new path of thoughtless thoughts unfolded in her mind- a nudge from the subconscious.

Unknowingly, unconsciously, people are doing the same things over and over- even if how different it looks from the outside. Some people chase and do a lot of things in their life -A person who is a merchant today, might become a soldier later. The same person might become a musician after that-but still, after all this- the void inside, remains the same. That's what makes people jump into spirituality at a certain stage - and yet, that too is just another hole dug. By the time they bury their previous garbage in it, their minds will clog with new garbage. Inner consciousness is the only thing that would free people from garbage. All the thought patterns, the delusional amusements, compulsive habits-- all are garbage that keep you away from knowing your true self. A short-tempered carpenter, let's say he becomes an artist later; just becomes a short-tempered artist. He has the same garbage in different forms, wherever he reaches.

That night, Rinzen wrote in her diary:

From temple to temple

Master to master

Creed to creed

One dogma to another

I relentlessly kept on digging holes;

Night and day;

Being deaf to the truth that,

every hole dug,

barely helped to bury

the garbage from previous;

and nothing else.

Market

A week later- one day, it was afternoon and Rinzen was just about to finish her cleaning work at the library. As she was returning the cleansed mop and bucket to the temple janitor, suddenly Master Bankei appeared beside her. "Rin, accompany me to the market. I would appreciate a hand" Master said.

Rinzen was happy as well as curious- she wanted to see how the master interacted with the people around. All the zen schools she attended before, had masters who never left the temple. Besides all that, Rinzen was so happy that she got a chance to go out and see things. Rin dressed up and got ready in no time.

It was afternoon when Rinzen and her master passed the main gate. After an hour of walk through the beautiful hilly path, they reached the market, which is situated right in the middle of the town. A mighty military barrack stood tall at the entrance. The market street was cluttered; stacked with small and large shops; and the footpaths were conquered by vegetable sellers- turnips, garlic, soya beans, spinach, corn, onions and some leafy vegetable about which Rinzen had no idea.

As they walked through the street, Master asked "Rin, from where did you get this red silk scarf? It looks so expensive"

The red silk scarf that Rinzen flaunted on her shoulder as well as Rinzen herself became glad.

"Thank you. It was a gift from the Governor."

Bankei exclaimed: "Great. How did the Governor happen to gift you?"

"I participated in a philosophy puzzle competition conducted at one of my previous schools. It was seven years back. One hundred and twenty people participated, and I was the only one who passed the final levels." Rinzen majestically waved the silk scarf, reliving her proud memory.

"Your intelligence is honourable, kid."

Bankei bowed to his disciple, satirically impersonating the clergymen.

Rinzen: "Hehe"

"Well..." Rin continued. "This year too, a competition is being held. This time it is from the King's court of ministers. They have advertised the question already. The person who gives the best answer, will get a big prize from the King."

"Are you participating?"

"Of-course yes, I have been working on that question"

"What's the question?"

Rinzen cleared her throat. "Ahem.. it sounds like a simple one, but I know it is not since it is from the King's court. The question is about geometry. Four geometric shapes are given.

Triangle, Rectangle, Square and Circle. Out of the four, what is the speciality of circle. That is the question"

Bankei: "What answers have you found?"

Rinzen: "At first, I wrote to them that the surface of a circle is equidistant from its centre at all points, unlike the other shapes- needless to say that it is the first thing that comes to anyone's mind about a circle. Obviously, the same answer was posted by hundreds of people; and got rejected." Rinzen finished her sentence with a self-mocked smile.

Bankei: "Then?"

Rin: "I referred to all the geometry books in our library today morning. I made some calculations and found another interesting thing about circles- that a circle is a shape which has least perimeter, for a given area."

Bankei: "Pardon me, my math is very bad, kid. Can you please explain it in simple terms for me?"

Rin looked around for some time. She pointed her finger to the corner of the street and said:

"Master, do you see that army barrack over there? It is circular in shape. It fits 25 soldiers. Let's say it takes 100 bricks to build its outer wall. But if it has to be of any other shape, it will take more than 100 bricks-may be 110; may be 120; I need to calculate to say the exact figure. But it will be always more."

Bankei: "So that's why most barracks are round."

Rin: "exactly"

Bankei: "Impressive as always. Send this answer. You will win"

Rin: "With your blessings, Master"

Rin and Bankei reached the middle of the market. Bankei examined each shop, each fruit, vegetables before buying. Some of them bowed to Bankei, as they recognised the Master in him. However, most of the people were unconcerned -they weighed him just like any other person on the street.

"Market is always crowded with vendors. Be wary of what you need to buy, or else your time here will be wasted"

Rinzen heard that in her Master's ethereal voice. She understood that it wasn't about markets. It was about life.

On their way back, they happened to see a funeral procession passing nearby. Watching it, Bankei said:

"Everyone's journey ends like this. No matter how great they were"

Rinzen: "Yes"

"Kid, did you meditate on the story I told you yesterday" Bankei asked.

"Yes master. I understood it. That evening in the garden unveiled a lot of meanings to me."

"Then tell me what came to your mind"

"People do a lot of hard-work, unaware of the fact that it doesn't help to liberate them spiritually. After finishing one work, everyone reaches the starting point again, like in an infinite loop of digging holes to bury garbage. They might get material wealth, but in spiritual progress, they will be still standing at the beginning. Just like searching for a lost key in the wrong place. No matter how much time he spends and how much effort he puts, he will never find the key. The story is about meaningless hardwork."

"No"

A perplexed Rinzen, yearned for the master's commentary.

"Tell me Master"

Bankei: "The story is about time and courage"

"Time and courage?"

"Yes"

"How?"

"Just because there was light, he searched in the yard, although he knows that it is not there. Humans engage in worldly materialistic affairs again and again even though they know that all those aren't going to last long; and they do it merely because it is more accessible.

Rinzen: "Master, if people 'know' where they lost it, why don't they look for it there? What makes them search in wrong places?"

Bankei: "Because it frightens them"

Rinzen stayed mute.

Bankei: "Have you heard of a Buddha quote? "It is easier to win thousand battles than to win one's own mind" "The most frightening battle is when you turn inside. The toughest battle is the battle which your own mind gives you."

"People can engage in a lot of things, and can continue doing it till the end of their lives,- but to identify their soul's purpose and adhere to it, demands courage- that's when the real war begins. It frightens them, so they just keep on doing whatever that is comfortable and easy, constantly ignoring the inner self. It is like a person who gambles. He knows he is losing money every hour. He knows he gets nothing but losses from it. But still he would revolve around it, because he is so acclimatized to it that he cannot search in any other place for his treasure, than the gambling table."

"Everyone is in search of their treasures. That's what the journey of life is. And everyone knows that it lies in the dark; their own inner depths. Yet, knowing all this, they waste their time looking outside in the light. To look inside the darkest depths of oneself takes courage."

It was twilight when they came back. Oil lamps glowed on every pillar. Bankei went to the meditation hall and Rinzen went to cleaning duty. She had a lightness inside, which she never had before. She dipped the mop in water and swiped over the polished bamboo floor. There is no time for leisure in a zen temple. Everyone has a daily duty, and that has to be finished at any cost. Rinzen mopped the floor with all the volume of her mind. Letting her mind flow out to her hands like Yangtze in monsoon; an unstoppable flow- fierce and brave-straight out from the soul; at that moment, the comforting dark idols in her mind- fear, anxiety, insecurity, egocentric thoughts- all became dissolved- she saw nothing but the mop, and the floor; Like an artist with brush, Rinzen made blissful strokes on the floor, with the wet mop. The lemongrass oil smelling cotton mop scrubbed gently, as if it was kissing on the floor. Veils of dirt got wiped off. A veil of unconsciousness parted away from her mind as well.

Zazen

Several monks were seen seated in lotus posture, with their eyes closed- it is called Zazen. In the courtyard, in the hall, veranda and even in the bamboo grove situated just outside the compound. Rinzen, after finishing her chores, was walking in the yard with a thousand unfinished thoughts.

A tough looking elderly monk, walked nearby all those Zazened students, examining them. "What on earth is there to examine about a set of people sitting and doing nothing?" -Rinzen thought.

That was a warm day. Letting the sunlight embrace her, Rin sat on a corner in the veranda, leaning on to a pillar. "If there was no sun, humans would have had to build an everlasting fire-but how would one build such a fire? All the woods in all the forests won't be enough for that." It was Rinzen's thoughts that actually caught the fire. "May be the powder used in fireworks could fit the job- or that stone lacquer from deep wells used to make fire- it could meet the demand"- her mind climbed along the endless thought ladder. "But where should the fire pit be placed? One in each city may be-" ***"excuse me?"*** a firm voice shook her out from the thought chain. It came from a handsome young monk, standing near her. He carried a rolled-up mat in his arms, pressed against his hip.

"Yes?"

"That is my meditating spot you are sitting on. Can you please leave that space to me so that I can do my zazen practice"

"Oh, sorry" Rinzen hurriedly stood up, apologizing to him.

He spread the mat and assumed the meditating posture calmly.

"Why are you not meditating?"

"No one instructed me to do so." Rinzen had a bit of anxiety in her, while saying it, but she tried not to display it.

"Why did you join the temple?"

Rinzen: "I came here for enlightenment"

"Then why are you not meditating?"

Rinzen kept silent for a minute.

"I have practised focus meditation and mantras in my previous schools but I miserably failed at it-"

He continued: "Zazen is a great technique. It is about making us distant from our own mind, and all its compulsions and judgements. Zazen will create a superior consciousness inside us."

Rinzen: "I have heard of it"

"There are many masters who became enlightened through Zazen"

Not letting Rinzen say anything more, he asked: "You look like a confused person. Just leave everything in your mind, and would you sit here for some time? I will guide you to Zazen. Come on."

Rinzen now wanted to try it. She remembered master's words- "One must have the courage to pursue the inner treasure"

Rinzen sat near him. She kept her legs crossed and spine straight, as he instructed.

She closed her eyes.

"Do not fall asleep- be awake like a guard dog. Thoughts would continuously come up, like a festival procession- do not join it; but watch it like an observer from the above. That's how you attain the thoughtless thought."

His explanation was straight to the point. Rinzen got the picture of what Zazen is, and she felt very high about the young monk. She let her mind loose, letting the wild chain of thoughts untie. She pictured herself bridging above her mind. she looked at her mind:

"What all are here? A part of my thought is about the geometry question-another river of thoughts are bringing up my past times- the times I lost, the times I spent on unnecessary things-the opportunities I missed- another chain of thoughts about future-am I going on the right path now? "

"You are thinking too much" the monk said.

Rinzen opened her eyes. "How did you know?"

"I can see that. Your spine was bent. It means you were lost to thoughts- and not awake"

Rinzen said: "I was trying. And I saw myself- I think I was on the right path"

"It takes time, I will suggest a method. After closing your eyes, concentrate on an answerless question." The monk said.

"What?"

"A koan"

"Give me a koan"

He paused for a minute.

"Find how your face looked like before your parents were born."

Rinzen again closed her eyes, assumed a straighter stature. She then took a deep breath, slowly exhaled, and her mind momentarily got tuned to certain revelations - "If my father married another woman, or if my mother married another man, I wouldn't have been born. But is that the true beginning of my existence?" She started to find her first memory of herself. She went back to childhood- delved deep into even younger days-face of her mother and father glimpsed like reflected images in rippled water. But she had to keep away from images. She tried to pan away her concentration from those memories, but still processing it. After a few minutes of that tug of war, she started to see an image of herself, where she is not a human. She saw herself as radiating aura, a power without a form. She saw herself floating in a blue space, just above the human-life-happening arena called earth. Blue- the colour of mysteriousness. Colour of limitlessness. There she saw her parents, being brought up in different homes at far off places. For a glimpse of time, she felt like she was separated from all the life and its emotions, but it still kept creeping in, and so to maintain her higher level she had to struggle. She focused on goal. Her blood flow increased; her heart beat fast; fingers curled as if she underwent a shock- she was struggling.

"Stop it!"

Rinzen suddenly opened her eyes, as someone tapped on her back.

She opened her eyes to see Master Bankei.

"Who told you to guide her?"

The handsome monk now wore a confused look.

"Never try to initiate other students. You may go." The monk bowed down to the master and Rin both, rolled up his mat in a hurry.

"Rinzen, you come with me" Bankei commanded.

The young monk went to the meditation hall, and Rinzen followed her master.

"Master, why are you not teaching me any meditation methods" Rin asked.

"Is that why you went Zazen?"

"Yes. I searched my inner truth- my treasure. I advanced in it a bit. I was able to see me flying over the ground. That was the first time I have ever had such an experience."

"You were dreaming. You were just seeing artistic picturizations of the ideas you had in your mind, about soul entering a suitable womb, life, death and rebirth-the entire samsara-chakra."

"So, all those are wrong?"

"Whether it is wrong or not doesn't matter- when you start a practice, just see whether it will help you or not and whether it is real or unreal. Moreover, it will be tedious verifying such things. That's someone else's quest. Not yours. Use your time wisely- do not waste it looking through wrong windows."

Bankei walked to the backside of the compound. The back-gate was open, and he stopped there.

"Go and have a walk in the mountains. Come back only by the evening."

"Just a walk?"

"Just a walk. Concentrate on your footstep- listen to the nature. Don't even think of spirituality- just walk; don't walk like a human- walk humbly like an animal- feel the earth, and come back."

Rinzen walked through the open gate, to the open world.

She passed the bamboo groves. She passed the grasslands. With every step the forest became thicker and darker. Bizarre screeches of unknown insects started to fill the atmosphere instead of melodious bird calls. She walked past the shrub field and oak woods, the curious mountain cats and mysterious meditating owls. Some trees bore fruits, some didn't. Some were green, some were brown. Some had flowers, some had bare branches. Rinzen let her mind flow out of her. Her footsteps became rhythmic. Between her and the nature, there was nothing. All her senses lovingly imbibed the mother earth - and there were tacit expressions all around. A smiling cuckoo bird, a fallen tree with budding twigs on it, a silver carp swimming against the flow of an overflown stream- nature kept on showing her meaningful coincidences. Her subconscious mind involuntarily got in harmony with the world around.

An hour of walking passed. There was an open field, no trees but only shrubs. But there was a cherry tree in the middle. A perfect wayside resting spot. Under the cherry tree, Rinzen sat in a comfortable way, and it was the lotus pose. It just came to her unconsciously. Humans calculate and spend their riches- nature simply gives it out. A big pile of cherries lay there on the ground- fallen fruits. One seed in one fruit is enough to bring a new tree, but nature is so extravagant. Its blessings are unbounded. Immeasurable. Nature initiated meditation in her. She didn't know how and when her eyes closed. Even though sitting in an unknown place, the cherry tree, the forest, the sky, the soil beneath- everything felt familiar to her. Like a baby in mother's lap, her eyes closed effortlessly. But the inner eye was open.

Under that beautiful motherly cherry tree, nothing came to her other than the cool mountain breeze. Every breath felt like medicine. Every breath rejuvenated her- and a smile blossomed on her face. She became unconcerned about time.

"Thud"

A bunch of cherries fell down. Rinzen opened her eyes suddenly. She took a long breath, leaned on the tree trunk.

She was surprised to see a lump of wool beside her, almost twelve feet away. 'Did someone drop it while travelling'- Rinzen thought, and taking a second look, she realised that it was not a woollen cloth. It was a wolf sleeping. A big grey wolf.

Fear electrified her spine. "No one can run faster than a wolf. And I don't know how to climb a tree too." – terror induced thoughts terrified her in no time.

The wolf had woken up by then. He stood up, looking at her eyes, and made a low-pitched whine. And it didn't seem friendly.

Thinking of ways to escape and cursing herself, Rinzen stood up slowly. That was a safer pose- either to run or to climb the tree.

Wolf snarled.

Suddenly a fire ball from the sky fell infront of the animal. It was a cracker. And it exploded before touching the ground- the wolf ran back like a rat escaping to its hole. Rinzen turned her head back and saw three men. They carried bows and arrows, and gunpowder crackers. Despite carrying weapons, they seemed docile and pleasant.

The men came near her, and bowed.

"Thank you for helping me. I owe you a lot." Rinzen expressed her gratitude to her saviours.

"Are you from the temple?"

"Yes. I am from the temple." Rinzen said.

Their faces filled with reverence- and Rinzen was surprised to see that. Without letting her process the surprise, they requested her to visit their village. She agreed.

The village was only a short walk away. There were several huts, made with straw and bamboo- all with elevated floors. There must be flood in the monsoon times- Rinzen thought. There was a big hut at the centre of the settlement, which looked like a place of worship. It might be their gathering hall- Rinzen thought. One of the men rushed inside that hut. After few minutes, a lady came out of the hut. She had braided hair, and her head was covered with a variety of natural ornaments- river snail shells, beads of wood resin, multi-coloured feathers and crystals of unknown origin. She wore a long woollen coat which was black in colour. Her pleasant smile was the only thing that didn't make her look like a black magician.

"I am Bilou..I welcome you to our village"

The lady greeted Rinzen with high admiration.

"You are from Bankei's temple?"

"Yes"

"My son works as a guard there." Bilou said.

"Oh, does he?"

"His name is Mingze."

"Please take a seat inside" Bilou invited Rinzen to the hut.

Rinzen walked inside the hut, to see that it was surprisingly spacious. There was a big table, a few benches, and mats. Furniture as well as pillars - all were made of bamboo. Floor was made of timber.

Rinzen was given a bamboo glass full of sweet water. The lady, the hut, the honey mixed sweet water in the bamboo mug- everything had a golden tint. It didn't take long for the hut to get crowded with people. There was very little talking- but Rinzen could hear them murmuring. And no one dared to sit beside Rinzen, they all kept a respectful distance from her. One woman from the crowd suddenly came near Rinzen and kneeled. She carried her baby with her.

"Please bless my child. She is sick"

Rinzen: "I am not a Monk, I can't bless"

Bilou: "But you are from the temple"

Rinzen: "I am only a learner. Just a normal person."

Bilou closed her eyes and kept her palm pressing to her chest. She whispered to herself – "Zhengzheng de"

"I know true Monks are humble. Please bless our people."

Bilou said.

"We saw her power. Her meditative aura was attracting animals. A wolf came near her and slept like a baby for an hour. And only when she woke up from the meditation it became a wolf again." The men said to Bilou.

"But it was you who saved me!" Rin said to the men.

"No. We usually never go for hunting in that area. But today, for no reason I got an intuition that we must go to western side of the woods. After we saw you, I understood that it was your aura that called us. I have heard stories about Monks sending inner messages to far away people, inspiring them do some specific tasks. And we are happy that we were able to do that duty."

Rinzen had no way other than to bless the woman and her child. She touched the baby's head with both her palms, and wished her a good life with all her heart. A blessing can never be of any harm- even if it comes from a non-Monk. Rinzen tried to sanctify her helplessness with logic.

"What is the problem with your child?" Rinzen noticed something strange and she asked straight. The woman then sat near Rinzen, opened the woollen blanket to show her sick baby.

The baby was blue. There were mysterious patches of blue shade under her skin- on her forehead, ears, nose and some parts of arms and belly.

"She never stops crying. I am afraid some evil spirits are doing this."

"How old is she?"

"8 months"

"Looks like poison to me" Rinzen said.

Rinzen suddenly stood up, and got outside the hut. Few men and Bilou followed.

"Where do you take water from?"

"We now take water from the stream there" Bilou pointed westwards.

"Take me there" Rinzen ordered the men.

Like newly appointed bodyguards, they escorted Rinzen to the hillside stream. It was just outside the last hut of their village.

Rinzen took some water in her palm, smelled it. "This water isn't good."

The men looked confused. "But the water looks clear" One of them raised doubt.

"Only to the eyes. It looks clear because it flowed through pebbles and sand. But it doesn't make it really pure. There is something in the water that eyes cannot see. But I can sense its smell."

When Rinzen came back to the village, she inspected the big wooden tank which they used to store water.

"Collect charcoal from all the homes and put it in the tank. Change it every 4 days." Bilou nodded her head.

Back in the hut, few more people took 'blessing' from Rin. Someone lighted an incense stick. The whole place looked like a monastery for a few hours.

"I am not what you think I am." As the crowd dispersed, Rinzen said to Bilou. "I am just a normal human like you. You have completely misread me. I also have a lot of problems in mind. I am not yet a master of myself."

Bilou was still not ready to accept it. She attributed it to the self-effacing temperament of Buddhist Monks, right from the time of Bodhidharma. Bilou and her men felt protected in presence of their new Guru.

"It is time to return" Rinzen said.

Two archers escorted Rinzen back to the temple. It was past twilight when Rinzen reached her room. She put on new clothes, had her feet and palms rinsed in cold water, and rushed to the library, to finish the pages she started yesterday. After half an hour, bells rang. It was dinner time.

Rice and cabbage soup was the dinner. Overboiled sticky rice kept clinging on to the chopstick.

"Ahem." Rinzen looked to her right to see the handsome young monk.

"I am sorry about what happened today" He looked guilty as well as embarrassed.

Rinzen: "It is okay, I am good."

"I heard from the guards that you were sent to forest"

"Yes"

"What were you doing there? Did you meditate?"

"I was searching for my face before birth" Rinzen was calm while saying it.

"Did you find it?"

Rinzen remained calm. "Yes. I saw it."

"How did it look like?"

"Blue."

Discussions

Hao Chen, a senior monk, sat in a wooden chair, facing a group of people, gathered at the centre of the garden. Not everyone of them were inhabitants of the temple. People from other monasteries, schools, villages, were all welcomed as anyone who wanted to attend could utilize the opportunity. Debates and discussions in Bankei's temple were open to all. Such open discussions were a part of the curriculum in the temple.

Hao Chen stood up to begin: "We, as the monks of master Bankei's temple, are happy to be in touch with the people-we always leave the gate of this temple open, intentionally. The path of Zen, is not confined to any monastery; it will be visible in every sort of common life-if you have the eyes to see it."

Hao Chen bowed towards the crowd.

Pressing palms together, he continued: "With gratitude, let us start the session- anyone can come forward with a statement, or doubt, or a topic of interest, then we shall discuss it together" – finishing the line, Hao Chen settled down onto the bamboo chair, facing the people.

A young monk, from the middle of the sitting crowd, stood up:

"Greetings to all. I would like to make a statement that, the most wonderful thing in this world, is love"

Hao Chen: (clapping his hands) "Ow.! Rationalize your statement please."

Hao Chen carried a mysterious air around him. No one could ever read from his face, whether he likes or dislikes something.

The monk, who seemed confident and spirited, cleared his throat, assumed a firm tone and started to explain:

"Love is the base of everything. Love is what makes the world sustain its harmony. What I see around in this world is lack of love; that is the reason why there is so much war in this world. Love makes people share everything; other than defeating and capturing. That's what our kings are doing. They capture resources; they never share with love. Indeed, the world has enough assets for everyone to use. But since people lack love, they don't share, and kings capture it; spreading violence!! "

A majority of the people applauded. "So true"- someone said. An indifferent Rinzen sat among the silent faction.

Moderating the crowd by hand gesture, Hao Chen said: "Love is a wonderful thing. There is no doubt. But what you idealised, cannot be related to what you said."

"If we all loved each other, all those wars wouldn't have happened." The young monk countered.

Hao Chen smiled.

“You see my robe?” Standing up, Hao Chen waved his hands to himself, displaying his coffee-brown Zhiduo.

“Yes”

“There is lot of empty space in between the folds of this Zhiduo. Can I let a snake live there? NO! (chuckles). There are boundaries. In forest, if you closely observe, you can see that every animal lives in its own territory. We as humans, also should draw boundaries wherever required. Everyone needs their time and space. Only then we can bring harmony in the world, and inside us. We always keep the gates open, but not the doors- we have guards here. Not everyone you see around is lovable. Some of them might invade your house. Take away your land and assets; do barbarous things to you; we need to avoid it- So we fight. Kings do that for us. We pay taxes, and they give us security.”

That created a fluster in the crowd. Many raised eyebrows were seen. Murmuring sounds of a disappointed flock were heard. Unaffected, Hao Chen stood there peacefully, after finishing his speech, casually sporting a pleasant smile.

A young girl stood up from the crowd, and asked.

“So, you are supporting violence? A monk like you telling us this!”

Hao Chen: “For a flower to bloom, the plant has to be protected. Protection is not violence. It is responsibility.”

“Then what is non-violence? it’s a core principle of Buddhism” The girl shrugged her shoulders as she asked it.

Hao Chen: "It is a state of mind. A state of mind reached after years and years of awakening experiences. When your mind withdraws from everything that comforts you, fear disappears. A fearless mind doesn't dwell in the past or future- it is as tranquil as a forest stream- flowing calmly, embracing the present moment; that is called awakening. And non-violence, is a consequence of awakening."

A man from the crowd asked: "I have heard a lot of times about this- 'living in the present'. Well, frankly I have never understood what it means. Anyhow, our mind is composed of the things we have known in the past, and the expectations we keep about the future. Only if we remember the lessons learned yesterday, we can mould ourselves to face tomorrow. Isn't it the normal, wise way of living? By telling to 'live in the present', does it mean to forget everything and live a careless and lazy life?"

Hao Chen: "I am going to give you a gold coin. Tell me what you will buy with it"

Man: "I would buy a grain whiskey-or go for a trip in the ship. Or a coat-made of crocodile leather" the man listed a number of things that he fancied.

"There is a shop which sells children's toys at the southmost end of the market-I hope you have heard of it."

"I know the shop"

"Why don't you buy a toy from there?"

"Why should I buy a toy now…."

"Why not?"

"I am not a kid anymore. A toy is meaningless to me now- as simple as that"

Hao Chen: "But as a kid, you loved toys, did you? "

"Yes. Especially those cloth dragons and wooden roly poly toys- I loved them when I was a boy."

Hao Chen: "You awakened from the world of toys, as you became mature. Now all those toys that once you craved as a kid, are of no interest to you. As a matured man, you are crying not for toys- but for some other fancy things that you desire. If you happen to visit a toy shop, you would feel like standing amidst a pile of things that doesn't bother you- doesn't make your mind anxious about whether you could have one for you or not- or doesn't make you worry about not having one- you will stand there peacefully- unstirred- just as an observer- being there and detached at the same time- living in the present. That's how an awakened person sees the whole world. For spiritually awakened persons, the whole world becomes a used toy- there is nothing more to take from it- nothing left to know about it- they simply remain aware of it, pleasantly observing the world- being in each and every moment. An awakened person's mind is the strongest wall in the universe- because it is impervious to the sharpest of weapons that no other person could endure- depression from the past and anxiety about the future."

There was a calm and contented applause from the audience.

The discussion continued. Another man from the crowd stepped in. The man looked weary- his frail shoulders were trying hard to hold his body straight. He spoke with difficulty.

"Last week, my wife left me and found another life. I am struggling to overcome it. "

Hao Chen answered: "When did you meet her for the first time?"

"Three years ago."

Hao Chen: "So, four years ago, she was not with you; but you were happy, right? Your mind knows how to stay happy without her believe in it. And move on."

Finishing the line, Hao Chen with a smiling face, said- "Next"

Another man stepped in.

"I wonder why art is so enjoyable. When we see a man playing a role, we know that it is not real, but we still feel the emotions conveyed as if they were real. A painting of a mountain, is never like the real mountain. The details of the real mountain that we see with our eyes, will never be seen in a small painting. But still, we like to see paintings. Same happens with any form of art. So, my doubt is this. Why is art so enjoyable?"

Hao Chen smiled. "Now this is a great question. Anyone to answer it?"

Several answers came in.

"What we like is the skill of the painter. When we see a painting, we feel contented, because we appreciate the skill of the painter" – A man who identified himself as a fisherman said.

"I don't like paintings at all. If you want to see a mountain, you can go and see it actually. Why would you waste time painting it?" – an old man declared.

Several opinions followed. Rinzen, who was quiet until then, stood up and said "Art is a journey to one's inner self"

Hao Chen, hearing this, clapped his hands.

"Now tell us more". Hao invited her.

She began – "When you see a mountain, you see a mountain, that's all. But when you see the beautiful sketch of a mountain, it invokes the impression of the mountain you have inside you. The sketch need not be the exact copy of the real view. But it invokes memories, and all those good memories you have about a beautiful mountain. And that is what we call art. It can make you experience more happiness than the real thing."

"Tell us more" The old man demanded.

Rinzen continued – "Take the case of a skit. In the skit, the actors depict a lot of life situations. Say grief, happiness, anger... and all these emotions are not unknown to the viewers. We all have had such situations in our life. We all have experienced sadness and happiness, lust and anger; achievement and disappointment; but when a person acts it infront of us for a short time, we get to observe it from a distance; its different, because when we had it in our own life, we couldn't observe it because we were so involved in it- we were a part of it; we were lost in it. Nonetheless, all those gets buried deep inside our minds, as imprints of memory. And while watching a play, we see those things from the depths of our minds getting portrayed- and there, you are simply a viewer- you know it's not happening to you; but you are experiencing it, from a different perspective. In simple words, you are watching life, from a distance. That's a delightful experience. That's art. It is an inward journey. "

The crowd clapped. Hao Chen came to the centre.

"That was a worthy talk. We are obliged, Rinzen" saying that, he bowed down to the crowd.

To the crowd, he said: "Rinzen just told us the basic principle of awakening- "Staying away from life, while living it"- The discussion is over. I thank everyone who gathered here"- Hao Chen bowed.

Crowd bowed back, and dispersed.

A Discovery

Bell rang- it was lunch time. In the temple, food timings were vastly strict, because the food that has been kept unused for a long time was considered not good for eating, and hence no person was allowed to eat late or early. And whether the incumbents who get late to the dining hall gets food or not, was left to the mercy of those security guards and the monk on kitchen duty for the day. The rosewood floored dining hall had the space to accommodate all the residents. A monk from the kitchen would ring a bell hung outside the hall- it was meant to notify the food time, and all the inhabitants would stop doing their chores, and show up at the hall without delay- however, the bell also used to invite a cluster of frequent visitors- neighbourhood cats. Felines were never driven off; master Bankei wanted to keep a dedicated corner in the yard to feed them.

Rinzen walked past the huge mechanical clock installed in the courtyard. It made a thud sound every hour and some monk would keep track of the number of thuds, starting from morning. The clock was made in Europa, and was bought to the temple by some wealthy government official of the King's court. Rinzen was seeing such a clock for the first time She was only familiar with water clocks. When Rinzen came to the dining hall, lunch had already started- clinking sounds of ceramic cutlery and bowls filled the air. Chef stood at the end of the hall, watching everyone. The soya chunk soup tasted mild, since Zen temple kitchens usually abstain from making food too spicy. Rice balls, dumplings and steamed Gai choy with tofu were the main course. Salted vegetables were kept in a bowl on every table. As Rinzen relished the rice balls with some soy sauce, she noticed a girl sitting at the far end, looking at her and smiling. She waved her hand to Rin, as if she were a fan. Rinzen smiled back at the girl, as she took a few dumplings to her bowl. The bland white dumplings felt tasty when she coupled it with pickled mushrooms.

Rinzen cleaned her bowl and the bamboo chopsticks and returned them to the monk on duty. Monks on cleaning duty stayed back at the hall. A few monks were feeding the cats, and some students joined them- they bribed the cats with those dumplings and tofu they smuggled from the dining hall in order to pet them for a while. Rinzen too had a liking towards cats because she believed that cats are the most contented animals on earth. That was however, true according to the mythology as well. The ancient cat named Li Shou, was entrusted with looking after the world. And all cats were given the ability to talk also. But gradually they forgot their duty and became pleasure seekers, running after mice, relaxing under the morning sun, playing and sleeping. Eventually they were dethroned and humans took their role. That's how humans started to talk and became the leaders of the planet. But to Rinzen, cats seemed to be still the bosses. How can it not be, since where there is a cat, there is a human trying to pet it and win its love- “haha” Rinzen laughed inside, as she walked to the library.

Entering the library, she found a comfortable seat, placed her paper and quill pen there, and started to search the geometry section. Fortunately, she found a few, including Euclid and Pythagoras. There were a few students in the library. Books from all around the world were stacked on huge wooden shelves; there was no librarian though. Any incumbent of the temple could use the library, at any time- even midnight. A guard, in charge of library would stand at the door; a namesake security. As Rinzen devoured pages one after the other, a girl came near her.

“Hi. I am Kathina. I am a student here too. I heard you at the discussion yesterday. That was remarkable” the girl bowed down to Rin. Wearing a purple Ruqun and straw shoes, she had all the effortlessness and energy of a scholarly teenager.

Kathina was the same girl who waved to Rinzen at the dining hall. Rinzen recognized her but she was not in the mood for a chat. Discouraging further talks, Rinzen settled it with a gentle pleasing smile and a thanks, then continued her reading.

“I didn’t expect to see you reading science! I thought you were an artist” saying that, Kathina sat near Rinzen.

“I like all subjects.”

“So, you like science.”

“Ofcourse.”

“I would like to ask you something about numbers. What are they actually?”

"In my view, numbers represent quantity, to put in simple words. We need numbers because we cannot record quantities in our memories and communicate. "

"Yes. I know that 3 apples are three apples, and if I have 4 more apples, there will be 7 in total."

"Ya, that's all. If you have a big bunch of apples, and you have to give it to someone else, you just have to count it once. Then you can call it as 1000 apples. The word thousand is its count, it helps you to communicate the quantity, without counting every time."

"Counting to 1000 is tedious"

"That's why we have mathematical operations. Just count to 100, and make a box. Batch 10 such boxes. Problem solved."

"Hmm, so numbers represent a physical quantity, hum?"

"Yes...language of physical world- math"

"But- I was thinking. I had 3 apples. But I lost 2 apples. Then," -Rinzen completed: "then you have 1 apple"

Kathina explained- "No, no, Rin, that's not what I meant to say...it's like, ok, I had this thought in my mind for a while...hmm, let me explain it to you with the help an example, ahem"

Suppose I have 40 apples. I always keep 40 apples at home, say. I give 2 apples to a friend. Now I have 38 apples.

"Yes. That's exactly what I said earlier!"

"You said numbers, all those mathematical rules; everything represent some physical reality, right. But I was thinking, how difficult it would be to mathematically express the situations that we are in; our mental states. “

Rinzen crossed her arms and looked at Kathina, with a raised eyebrow- a gesture that Rin does, particularly at times when she gets nudged by her insightful subconscious mind.

“What are you getting at?”

“Isn’t it like.. you can say that I have 38 apples, or I have 2 apples short of 40. Both means the same right”

Rinzen dug her deep mind for a second.

“Negative number!!” – “I have read about it”

Kathina felt it, but she had never heard of it.

Rinzen: “Negative numbers have been conceptualized in China for centuries...But in 7th century, which is almost 800 years back, a mathematician named Brahmagupta from India, coined the rules of negative number math. I have read about it in my previous school’s library. But since it is not taken into common math and number system yet, it simply remains in books.”

Rinzen was a bit surprised, that a student much younger to her came up with such a great thought. Although a math teacher, Rinzen had never thought of numbers in such a manner. An innocent Kathina, wanted to know more about it- “so, this kind of math represents what? “

Rinzen: “in worldly meaning, it is the sense of loss, you can say. Even when you have 38 apples, but in reference to 40, it is -2. But when you reference it to nothing-or zero, it is 38.”

“So, it exists in our mind”

“It depends on the scales you have set. Reference points- from where you look at things. Same applies to life also. When you look at your life from the perspective of all the things you had earlier and now lost, all you see will be negative. But when you look at the things you have in your life, however small those be- doesn’t matter; look at it from a perspective of you having nothing- then everything would seem positive.

“You are so intelligent, Rin. I admire you. I wish to become like you some day.”

Rinzen: “You are far more intelligent than me! I had the knowledge, so I just picked it up from my memory. But you observed something, thought of it, related it to what you know, theorised it up inside your head. That’s what real intelligence is. Some people can read a whole library and store everything inside their head. They may remember and recite; but that’s mechanical- that’s ‘dead knowledge’. Observation and imagination and correlation are far more important than that- and you have it, Kath “

Kathina bowed, and left the place. Rinzen returned to her reading, but after a few minutes, her mind took a turn. Kathina was nearly 8 years younger to Rinzen. She pictured herself as a younger Kathina, and thought about the chances of her discovering the concept of negative numbers. She couldn’t find it- and it was unclear what she felt was fear or a slight anger.

With a disturbed mind, Rinzen walked out of the library and headed to her room.

Soup

Knowing that it was the day of kitchen duty, Rinzen showed up at the kitchen, well before evening. Chef was busy with dinner preparation. The kitchen was a large hall, with a wide, greyish stone counter at the centre, which looked messy-covered all over with powdery finger marks and small dunes of millet flour- as if shouting out loud that the kitchen is a busy one. Next to the counter there was a partition, made of brick masonry, on which oil lamps were seated. Hanging shelves had flavouring agents and oil kept in cork sealed tight glass containers. Rumbling noise of the boiling pots echoed between those blackened walls. Wiped floor gave out the smell of lemongrass oil. If it is a kitchen, it must have lemongrass smell- the most sought-after disinfectant cum air freshener. The chef stood near the soup pot, waiting for it to boil, holding a stirrer in his hand. He was a grey-haired man, must be in his 60s. There were about a dozen of bamboo boxes, containing vegetables. Spinach, bottle gourd, beans, Gai Lan, Bok choy-all freshly plucked from the yard. Apart from the vegetables, the only thing colourful in that blackened kitchen hall were those yellow, red, white tall ceramic pots with crocheted jute lids, placed beside all four walls which contained salted mushrooms, pickled cabbage, sauces, and sometimes fermented soybean paste.

Chef directed his stirrer towards the corner of the kitchen, and showed a karate-chop like gesture, instructing Rinzen to go and cut the vegetables.

Rinzen's duties involved cutting vegetables, cleaning utensils and whatever job the Chef bestowed. It was the first time Rinzen attending kitchen, but the chef didn't ask any questions to her or initiate a chit-chat, although Rinzen expected it- her first day was just another day for the chef. The rotating duty assignment among incumbents gave one person every day, to the kitchen- just a normal daily routine stuff for the chef.

Nodding to the boring chef, she walked towards the corner, to find a wooden chopping pad near a sharp knife, and a bamboo basket full of fresh young Bok choy, not more than six inches. One cut at the white stem part, another cut above it, and one more cut right below the leafy part- that was enough to make them mouth sized.

"Pass me that lemon" Chef said while stirring the soup.

Rinzen opened a bamboo box, to see fresh baby green lemons. Surprisingly, all of them were so perfectly spherical, that they looked like marbles.

"I don't need the entire basket! Just pick one. Soup is getting thicker" Chef hurried. Rinzen took one lemon and gave it to Chef. With a pointed knife, he simply made a hole in the lemon, and dropped it into the boiling soup.

"Why don't you just cut it in half and squeeze?" the surprised Rinzen asked.

Chef (raising his eyebrows): "I don't impose. I just surrendered it to the soup, and the soup will take the right amount, at the right time."

A few seconds of silence followed. Rinzen couldn't find from where that came from- a cool mountain breeze pampered her amidst the smoky kitchen air. Some conversations lead her to silence; and silences give birth to wisdom. Rumbling noise of the steam pot suddenly became musical. At the moment, a mysterious calmness lifted away all her turmoil- and she left the soup to boil, waiting for it to get cooked in its own terms.

Coming back to room, Rinzen took out a sheet of her mulberry bark paper, adding to the diary, she wrote:

Hot boiling soup called life

Just add the ingredients

Nothing more; nothing less

Meddle not; hurry not;

Leave it free,

Luscious flavours would come up

Rinzen lay on her bed for some time. A hurricane of thoughts shook her mind. She suddenly stood up, and proceeded to her table with a geometry book in hand. She needed to find the answer for the contest.

A few hours passed. Almost all theories to her knowledge had been used. She thought about the spiritual parallels of those theories. But couldn't reach a conclusion.

What could be the speciality of a circle? Rinzen thought. Rin's mind entered a debate.

In the imaginary debate, Rinzen faced a great philosopher-mathematician. The debate is at the hall of king's court. All the ministers, the King himself, and eminent professors from universities of the region are present.

"Why is circle even important? I don't like that shape. There is nothing to it other than some doomed meanings" Rinzen established.

"Shall we know your explanation of it?" a mathematician sarcastically commented.

All in the hall yearned to know what the young girl had to say. Somebody from the crowd murmured that she is the winner of the Governer's award. The crowd honoured her. Now it is the time Rinzen show her knowledge to everyone.

A confident Rinzen, faced the crowd and divulged:

"A circle is a loop. It's a symbol of meaningless things humans commit in their life; lack of progress; no matter how far you have gone, you come back to the same point after some time. Great King Alexander died with nothing in his hand, just like the time when he was born, after that glorious career as a great King. Isn't it the ideal representation of human life?"

"A great philosopher", "at this young age" -voices from the crowd said. The audience applauded her.

Rinzen saw a convincing smile on the mathematician's face.

A loud knock at the door relieved her from the imaginary world.

She opened the squeaky wooden door. A rigid faced tall security guard stood there.

"Master Bankei is calling you. Meet him at the hall." As soon as he finished talking he left.

Rinzen got dressed up, locked her door and headed through the dark corridor, to the central hall. The floor was dirty- it needed a cleaning. Rinzen wondered how fast the dirt comes again despite the frequent mopping.

She had taken a few sheets of paper and pen with her- although now she knew that writing was not needed in Bankei's class; but still she wouldn't go without it; she had seen practitioners who drink tea and chew tobacco round the clock. This was just paper. She had approved it as a part of her trait. A harmless addiction.

Upon reaching the hall, Rinzen saw Bankei leisurely sitting on a chair. That was the first time she saw her Master like that.

Rinzen bowed. Bankei did a blessing hand gesture.

"Kid, your unhinged thoughts are radiating in this entire temple. You better stop it" – "Haha" – there was a mysterious giggle at the end of it.

Rinzen couldn't believe her ears. "How did you know I was thinking?"

Master continued: "Flowers in the garden told me, that they can't sleep because someone's energy is reverberating insanely. Your thought energy is polluting the whole atmosphere; slowly disturbing our harmony."

That also had Bankei's majestic chuckle following.

Rinzen's eyes bulged. She was wordless. "The master knows everything." Rinzen's mind wondered, but was doubtful as well at the same time.

“At what stage of spiritual progress do you become capable of reading the minds of others? I am asking out of my academic interest, master.” Rinzen asked.

“When your mind vibrates the least, you sense every other vibration around you”

Suddenly the knowledge seeker inside her woke up.

“So, can you sense ghosts? How can you explain them? Do they exist even?”

Bankei smiled. “You just can’t stop feeding your brain, huh?”

“I would like to know them. That’s a grey area of knowledge to me. I haven’t read anything substantial about it so far”

“I will tell what I know” Bankei started explaining:

“All suppressed desires are ghosts- whether they have a living body or not- desires are part of your souls; part of your consciousness- born from your perception of the world around- and some people’s desires persist even after the body is lost- they don’t know their body is lost; they remain unseen, unheard, unattended- absolutely helpless-but still hopefully waiting for their desires to get fulfilled someday, although their times have ended”

“But why are they depicted as dangerous?”

“When helpless humans are left uncared, unheard and unattended forever, they transform- that’s how angels are born. That’s how demons are also born. Unfortunately, the former seldom occurs”

Rinzen took a deep breath.

She told Bankei: "Master, I feel perplexed. Part of me tells that I must go and acquire more knowledge and prove myself and earn a place in this world- part of me tells to withdraw from all those fanciful things and seek the spiritual path. I am constantly being churned in the middle of this tug of war between what I want and what I need"

Bankei continued: "Do not take yourself too seriously, kid; otherwise your mind will never settle"

Rin: "But I have my own life goals, like every seeker… how can I remain calm when I have a war inside?"

Bankei: "When the war is in the war-field, you kill your enemy; but when it is in your mind, you kill yourself"

Bankei: "I will tell you a story. Listen carefully!" Bankei began in his calm voice.

> *One fine day, a neighbour came to Nasruddin. "Our house is so crowded," he complained. "We can't tolerate it anymore. Can you give me solution to it?" "Yes, I can help," Nasruddin said. "But you will have to obey my instructions exactly." The neighbour agreed. "Listen- Bring all your sheep, chickens, and donkeys into the house." Although confused, the neighbour left for his home and did what he was told. A week later, the neighbour told Nasruddin, "Nasruddin, it just made the problem worse" "Calm down, I know that," said Nasruddin. "Now, send the sheep outside." "Now it is better than before," said the neighbour a week later. "Well, now you may send the chickens out." "Now it's even better," the neighbour said next time. "Send the donkeys out too." Next time, Nasruddin's*

neighbour came to him with a blissful smile on face. "Thank you, Mullah Nasruddin!" he said. "Now there is so much space in our house!"

Rinzen understood something. But she waited for master's delineation.

Bankei continued:

"The 'house' in the story is mind. Mind is the first and foremost house of every human being, right from the birth till death. Even the things that are seen or heard or felt for a short period of time gets lifetime free stay in that house. Finally, the house gets crowded with infinite number of unwanted members, making it difficult for the owner to even sit inside the house. Gradually, the owner gets kicked out. That's your situation. "Lost in the crowded mind". Your mind is clogged with griefs about the past and anxieties about the future. Do not let the past and future poison you, dear kid"

Rinzen: "In the previous day's discussion, Master Hao Chen said something similar. So, Nirvana is living in the present moment-and that is the ultimate spiritual state, am I right, master? "

Bankei looked right into her eyes.

"Haha… as I said earlier, you are using your head too much, kid…Okay, I will tell you a Zen story."

A person came to a zen master, seeking meditation teaching. The master trained him for a few months, and asked him- "How do you feel now?"

He said: "A lot better. Now I see my mind is so clear, no compulsions no anxiety. I feel wonderful"

"Leave it" the Zen master said.

Then the master trained him for a year.

"Now how do you feel?"

"I feel a blissful emptiness. There is nothing left in me, other than the present moment"

"Leave that too" master said.

Bankei bowed to Rinzen, and said "You will get to know more later, kid. Now go and have dinner"

Rinzen had subtle awakenings inside her. Using the mind while not using it- isn't it almost equal to living while not living?

She headed to the dining hall. But she didn't reach there. Hunger of soul had conquered hunger for food. Every time the master spoke to her, she felt like being taken to the verge of enlightenment and coming back in less than a second- like being caught in a wave. Afterwards her mind would try to bring back the same state, but it was tougher than recollecting a forgotten dream. Rinzen sat leaning on a pillar, somewhere in the long veranda. She didn't notice the time that passed. She didn't see the people who passed. She didn't hear the dinner bell.

It was almost midnight when she woke up. She couldn't figure out whether it was her body or the soul which took rest. She came back to her room and sat on her chair, started reading a book.

And there was a knock at the door.

"At this time who is it" Rinzen wondered.

Opening the door, she saw a guard, carrying a tray full of food.

"Dinner" he said.

Rinzen (surprised): "Thank you so much."

"I am Mingze. Bilou is my mother."

Rinzen remembered. Excited, she said: "I wanted to find you but I forgot your name as soon as I came back that day. Sometimes my memory is too bad."

"It is alright. Your medicine worked. The baby is fine now. Not only the baby- everyone who had stomach ailments are fine now. Did you study medicine?"

"Oh, good to hear that. I haven't studied medicine- I read about it in some book."

"About babies turning blue?"

"No.. it was a book about the poisons in water and how to treat it."

"How did you know that it is from water?"

"It was an intuition."

"The ocean is also blue." Saying that, the guard took a small linen pouch from his pocket and gave it Rinzen.

"This is a gift. A part of my hard-earned treasure from my ocean days."

Rinzen opened the pouch, to see black coloured tiny spherules.

"What is this?"

"Black gold- that's what they call it. It has peculiar flavour. Try it."

Rinzen took one and chewed- and that was instant comfort.

"I have heard of it. But never seen it"

"People in Europa buys it in large quantities. It is the best spice they say."

"It will be nice if we put it in our soup- I think" Rinzen said.

"It goes good with everything"

"How did you get it??"

"I was a sailor in Admiral Zheng He's ships. We travelled west- pretty far west."

"Interesting" Rinzen said.

"I got this from the coast of Malabar. All of the world's black gold is from that place. Europeans trade ship-full of quantities every time they visit. I had a friend in the port of Ko-chih. I got this from him."

It was the first time Rinzen was meeting a sailor. Seeing that Rinzen wanted to know more of his stories, Mingze sat on the bed and asked Rinzen to eat the food.

Noodle soup and sauteed broccoli- and a small portion of salted mushroom.

"Tell me more of it" Rinzen said as she ate.

"There were three ports- the first one we reach is Coilum. After one night and one day sailing from there, Ko-chih can be reached. After one more night and day, their northern port called Ku-li is seen. All are big ports. Unimaginable amount of trade happens there every day."

"How does that place look like?"

“Everywhere there are coconut trees. And people cultivate them it in large numbers too. Some people have more than 3000 coconut trees in their farm.”

“Coconut?”

“It is a tall tree. With big fan like leaves. Leaves and fruits are only at the top. There are no branches.”

“I see”

“Admiral liked Ko-chih so much, and so we had more trade with Ko-chih. The emperor once sent a stone tablet with an inscription made by himself.”

“Emperor Yingzong?”

“ No.. Emperor Yongle.”

Rinzen heard all of it with excitement. Sea voyagers always bring interesting stories with them.

Before leaving, Mingze told her stories about pirates and sea monsters that he heard from Arabs. Mingze had learnt a little Arabic as well as Portuguese.

Finishing the dinner, she took her toothbrush. Made of oakwood, it had horse hair bristles- one of the finest tooth cleaners available. Salt, vinegar and cloves made her toothpaste. Clove left her mouth aromatic even after a thorough wash with cold water.

Rinzen came back from the bath, placed her footwear to rest, and sat on her bed for a while. Amidst the crowded house, her tired body demanded a quiet rest. Chattering for the day has come to an end -She fell asleep.

Legs

A wealthy merchant came to visit Master Bankei. He disclosed that he wanted to know something from the Master. Rinzen directed him to Master's chamber.

Bankei opened his eyes as soon as they stepped inside.

"What is it that brings you here?" Bankei inquired in his soft voice, compassionately.

"I want to learn meditation"

Bankei: "You are welcome. You can join this temple tomorrow morning. Stay here for 41 days. You shall not indulge in any other affairs"

"I am afraid I cannot spend too long here, Master"

Bankei simply raised his eyebrows at him.

Merchant: "I do exhaustive work night and day building my trade. However, I am an admirer of ancient Zen wisdom; hence I admit the truth that I cannot take all this wealth beyond my graveyard. Indeed, I need to learn a meditation technique which I can practise every day"

"Well, how much time can you spend every day?"

"My lord, it would be great if you teach me a technique, which requires the least time. Like 10-15 minutes a day. And in 10-12 months of practice, I should become a spiritual person. Guide me Master"

Bankei closed his eyes for a minute, and started: "I will tell you a story. This is a Nasruddin Mullah story, a Sufi Master who lived Turkey in the 13th century; 200 years before us."

> *A man saw Nasruddin standing near the lake, putting something into the water. He decided to see what exactly was going on there. As he approached, he saw that Nasruddin was pouring milk into the lake, with a spoon. "Why are you doing this?" asked the man. "It has only started" Nasruddin explained. "My aim is to turn the whole lake into milk one day" "What are you saying? That's impossible!" said the man. "Yes, I know it is," Nasruddin agreed. "But just imagine- how wonderful it would be!"*

A spoonful of milk, even if poured every day, will never turn the lake into milk. And to make a man spiritually awakened, is like trying to turn the universe into milk. To deal with a human, is equal to dealing with the universe.

The Merchant left.

Rinzen asked her Master: "Master I am confused"

"You are always confused. You can't even select a lemon from the lemon box"

Rinzen was so eager to get her question answered, that she ignored it and asked straight away:

"Master, you taught me that hard work is not the key in spiritual journey. But on the contrary, you rejected that merchant, telling him that it would take more effort and dedication than what he proposed, to achieve the spiritual light- isn't it like you were indirectly saying hardwork is the key?"

Master smiled.

"A man stands on two legs. A horse stands on four legs. A spider on eight; centipede on a hundred. But there are some humans who walk on a thousand legs. Whatever new thing they learn, just becomes a new leg. A spoonful of milk put into the lake, becomes the lake, and not the lake becomes milk. That man already has a thousand legs- legs are patterns of mind; Mind creates patterns of anything and everything we feed to it- and it won't let you break out of those patterns. If I teach him a spiritual practice, he will get one more leg as an accessory, and that's it- the mind will learn the pattern, and it will simply make him do it every-day, under the watch of his own delusions. How can one attain the ultimate freedom, if one is not ready to break free from the comfortable prison of patterns the mind sets up? If you feel that spirituality and those practices are a part of you, understand that it is just a pattern-a routine; a misconception. There were several people who spent years and years on techniques to attain enlightenment- chanting mantras, breathing techniques, martial arts, yoga- but still failed, for their minds were stuck to patterns. Spirituality shall not become a part of you; you should become a part of spirituality.

Rin sharpened her eyes and ears. “How does one become a part of spirituality?”

“Through surrender -- an unconditional surrender. Your mind shall invariably be in tune with your inner light. Surrendering yourself completely, whatever you start to do will become your spiritual practice- let it be yoga, Kung fu, cleaning the floor, gardening- whatever you do, it will instinctively turn into a meditation. Bridge above all those that are there in your mind. One who surrenders, never worries about how much hard-work he has done, how much effort he has given; he will imbibe the light of Zen, at the right time, just like the soup taking juice from the lemon”

“Can you explain it further, Master?” Rinzen wanted more of it, to complete the connect-the-dot puzzle of her inner mind. “When you said ‘surrender’, it seems so easy to do- is that all what’s required?”

“Easiest words constitute the hardest things often” Bankei calmly responded. “I will tell you one more story—listen, kid”

Nasruddin woke up from his sleep, as he heard the sound of a thief outside. In no time he ran outside, carrying a stick in his hand, he surveyed all around the yard. But he saw nobody, but he was sure the thief was hiding somewhere. Then he looked into the well. And he was quite convinced that he saw a man’s face in the water. “Foolish thief!! Now how do you think you are going to escape huh? Now stay there until I show you to everyone” Nasruddin shouted down at the thief. He then ran to the house and hurried up his wife:

"I will go call the guards!" he said. "You go and keep an eye on him. He is in the well!" His wife rushed outside and looked down into the well- and she was startled. "Oh, I see another one!" she yelled. "I think he must have brought his wife with him as an assistant."

Whatever we do, we see ourselves in it- that is the principal obstruction in spiritual awakening to all humans. Without overcoming it, one cannot become a part of spirituality. That's the difference between childhood and adulthood- when you become mature, suddenly a new ego comes standing in the middle of you and your own inner world. Enlightened masters often act childlike –you might have heard of it. Ego is the most cunning entity in the world- it may appear to you in the form of anger, hatred, jealousy- you already have conditioned your mind that those are bad. But what even more deceptive is that, it can also exist in you as morality- thinking good, doing good, making others happy, helping the needy, wishing good unto others, sacrificing, donating things- any such framework.

"So, then what is actually good and bad?"

"You will know it from me when you are ready. Now it is not the time"

"How does a person who has surrendered himself, behave like? I cannot relate it with anyone I have seen so far."

Bankei looked at her with compassionate eyes.

"Have you heard of Archimedes"

"Yes. He explained the law of buoyancy" Rinzen said.

"He was entrusted with finding an answer to a difficult question. He kept on thinking, and he was so filled with it, that he overcame himself. The moment he discovered the answer from his own inner world, he acted like a mad man, walked out nude on the street, celebrating it. At that moment he didn't see himself. All he saw was the discovery."

"So, those Greek thinkers were all Zen masters too?"

Bankei: "The essence of Zen is that, as I told you before, everything that you do surrendering yourself to, will become a spiritual practice. Nothing else matters."

A Visit

"You have a visitor" A security guard apprised Rinzen, at her door.

"Who?"

"How do I know? It's a woman-that's all I know" the security guard expressed his irritation and walked away.

Rinzen had just finished her study and was resting. A curious Rin dressed up slowly. She had not told anyone about this temple, and hence never expected a visitor.

At the hall, there stood Pema, Rinzen's old friend.

Pema confidently smiled when she saw Rin. Her silky-linen Yuanlingshan was of sparkling red colour. It had a four clawed dragon badge beautifully etched on it- like a fine artwork. Her linen-silk shoes made absolutely no sound while pressing on to the floor.

"How did you find me?" Rin was a bit worried about the visit.

Pema: "I can if I wish. I have my sources" the gorgeous looking Pema majestically waved her hand. Pema looked like she had everything that Rinzen fancied.

Rinzen invited Pema to the visitor's area in the main hall. They both sat facing each other, on bamboo chairs. Every movement of Pema radiated waves of Chrysanthemum nectar fragrance. The white lead powder coat on her face shined like glazed Qinghua porcelain.

"One night you left the school…where were you these five years?" Pema's tone had eagerness as well as authority.

Rin: "I went to the moon and came back. Had to visit some relatives there."

Pema sensed the sarcastic edge.

"I just came to see you- it took me a while to find out that you are here- Because I like you Rin- and I care for you. Tell me, what are you doing here? Are you teaching here?"

A nonchalant Rinzen said: "Studying."

Pema's eyebrows raised in disbelief. "What?"

Rin: "Yes. I am still a student."

Pema suddenly realized that it was meaningless to expect Rin to make a normal reply. However, out of the care and compassion towards her friend, Pema couldn't stop the words from her heart: "Dear Rin, if you want a job, I can get it for you. You don't have to prove anything to anyone- I know you are as knowledgeful as any professor in any university in this land. So, if you…" –

"NO" Rinzen intervened abruptly. You won't understand, Pema. Sorry."

"I know everything- your search, your journey; I understand. But you were so good at the school. You could have completed it."

Rin: "And then what? Everything inside me would have still remained the same"

Pema had nothing more to ask. After a few chit chats, she said goodbye. Rinzen walked her to the gate. Pema's guards awaited her. But they were not ordinary guards. They were soldiers. And the horse cart was not a carriage. It was a chariot with the emblem of ministry.

Pathways

The next morning, Rinzen woke up to silence. She didn't hear the birds, the subtle burning of incense wood or the chanting from the meditation hall. Sitting upright in the bed, she started to tie her messy hair. Once it was as silky as a Ferghana horse's coat. She saw her palms getting warts, once smooth skin becoming creased and dull. Like Eve of Eden suddenly becoming aware of her nakedness, Rinzen instantly felt herself grotesque. Such thoughts never had a place in her- even at the time of full youth. With a flustered mind, she walked out of the room, aiming to see Bankei. She didn't even hear her own footsteps- an agitated mind cannot be open to the nature around.

As expected, Bankei was seen sitting at the centre of the hall, like a stone statue, with his eyes closed.

"Master" Rinzen called.

Opening his eyes and gifting a blissful smile, Bankei greeted her with a quote: "No matter how good you are; you may see someone better –but the wise people never get upset about it, for it is the nature of the world"

"Was it for me? With all respect master, I am telling you that I have nothing to do with that quote"

Rinzen troubled to conceal her emotions.

Bankei: “Haha…just keep it in mind, kid. The only thing good to carry with you, are the quotes and the ideas – you cannot carry gold or sword, for you are a traveller in Zen’s path”

“hmm” Rinzen nodded.

“What about the competition, kid? Did you send your answer?”

Bankei asked Rin, as they leisurely strolled in the garden.

“It got rejected. Heard that a hundred people sent the same answer”

“I see.”

Master noticed an anxious Rin.

“You seem tensed. What is the reason, kid? “

Rinzen: “My friend Pema- she came to visit me yesterday”

“hm”

Rin: “She and I attended all the schools together. After school we parted our ways. She went for teaching in a school; and I went on my journey.”

Master: “What did she tell upon her visit”

Rinzen: “Nothing. She got appointed as literature expert in the King’s court of ministers. She was the one who told me that almost 100 persons sent that answer. Because she is one among the board members who scrutinise the answers. And that is how she found me out.”

Master: “Well, if you see her again, convey my greetings to her. She has acquired a great position at this age!!”

"Hmm." Rinzen seemed morose.

"I could have been in the same position... or some other equally high position. But see me now! I achieved nothing, despite having all that education."

Master: "You are knowledgeable and well read. You are good at math and literature as I can see. You can find a job easily if you set your mind on it, kid. It is not too late. However, I will tell you a story"

> *Nasruddin as a Sufi master, had become famous for his wisdom. As a result, people started to flock around him asking questions.*
>
> *One day, a visitor asked "Why does different people follow different paths in life? Why can't all of them follow one true path?*
>
> *Nasruddin smiled, and answered "It's actually for the good of all of us, that people follow different paths. Just imagine; if everyone chased the same path and arrived at the same destination, how boring this world would become!! Moreover, this world will overturn and we all will be doomed."*

Rinzen: "Maybe it is my problem. But I think it is time that I should be finding a position in the world that suits me, Master"

Master: "Have you planned applying to some university for a job?"

Rin: "Yes. I thought of going to Xi Jian; there is a school of literature and philosophy. I had written to them a year ago, and they replied recently."

Master: “I know that temple. One of my students is a master of martial arts there. What position did they offer you?”

Rinzen: “It seems they would place me as the library curator. Actually, that is a lower position for someone like me who has achieved the governor’s silk scarf award. But for now, I am not going to question it.”

Master grinned “You can, later.”

Rinzen said “Yes. Only a very few has gotten silk scarf award.”

“Undeniably.” Bankei bowed to Rin.

As the walk finished, Master went to the meditation hall. Rinzen went to library.

She read geometry and philosophy books one after other, in and out. She kept on making notes on her diary.

Garments

Rinzen was brooming the inner floors of the temple. Master suddenly appeared beside her. He carried a large cotton garbage bag on his shoulder.

"Rin, go and burn this garbage at any corner of the yard" Placing the bag on the floor, Bankei said.

"Yes, master"

Rin found a corner, arranged the burn wood, lighted a flame stick and made a fire. She emptied the garbage onto the fire. The weather so cold that day, that she felt comfortable near the fire. As she stood there waiting, she noticed something.

Among the garbage, there lay her silk scarf-being slowly burned.

She jumped on the fire, stomping vigorously, to put it out.

"My scarf! Oh, God" an agitated Rinzen, somehow managed to pull out the partially burned piece of her scarf. It is no more a scarf now. It's only a burnt cloth now- a piece of garbage.

"Why did he do this to me?" Rin growled in disappointment, as she darted to the temple.

"Do you know its value?" She roared at her master.

Her voice echoed in harsh resonance all around the meditation hall, but Bankei seemed unaffected.

"Are you really enlightened or are you a mad imposter? How could you do something so tricky and crooked? I don't want to know how you managed to get hold of my scarf, but I want to know why the hell did you trick me into burning my own prize; my most valuable achievement"

Bankei was calm, as if nothing happened. He said: "You cannot live without it?"

"Well how do you think I am going to earn my position in the world without it?" Rinzen sat defeated on the floor and almost fainted.

"The mind and your inner talent that made you win the contest is still there inside you. Nobody can burn it. So, do you believe in your inner strength, or in a piece of cloth?"

"But Master…."

"Your scarf is there at your room, wherever you kept it last" Bankei was as calm as a tranquil river.

Hearing this, Rinzen ran to her room. There she found her scarf, inside her shelf, exactly at the same place where she kept it.

Rinzen came back to Bankei, and bowed.

"What was the purpose of this bitter game, Master"

Bankei started "As always, I will tell you a Nasruddin story. Listen."

One day Nasruddin's wife was hanging clothes on the balcony for drying under the sun. Suddenly a gust of wind swept Nasruddin's shirt, whirled it for some time and dropped it on the ground. Seeing this, Nasruddin who was sitting in the patio downstairs, started laughing and said thanks to God aloud. His wife came downstairs, and asked "Hey, your shirt just fell to the ground. What is there to laugh in it and why are you giving thanks?"

He said "I just imagined how disastrous it would have been if I were in that shirt. God indeed saved me."

"Attires fall. But persons shall not. Will you get hurt if your shirt falls to the ground? No. Everything that you think is yours, is barely of the same value of a garment that you wear. All garments will fall; today or tomorrow. The positions you hold, things you own, your reputation among people, the achievements you made… everything might fall one day; but you shall not fall along with it. Do not live inside your garments; for the reason that you might fall and die along with it. Your true power lies within. Behold it, be proud and admire it; you will never fall."

Worlds shattered, worlds opened-inside Rinzen, as she came to the edge of her subconscious mind.

"I have questions to ask, master"

"Go ahead." Bankei said.

"I don't want stories anymore. I want unadorned disclosures."

Bankei nodded to it.

Rinzen: "What is good and bad?"

"The things that you do with awakeness are good; those which are not, are bad.""

Rinzen: "As simple as that? hmm, let me take an example- a person is awake all day; let's say he drinks wine in the evening-everyday; so that's the only time when he does bad deeds, and rest of the time all he does is good?"

Bankei: "After drinking wine a person becomes unconscious- we know that. But remember, it is without being drunk that every drunkard takes the decision to go to the bar. People are far unconscious well before they get drunk." Bankei finished the last sentence with a laugh.

Rin: "What does 'Awake' mean, then? "

Bankei: "Awake means being extremely true to one's self"

Rinzen's pale face struggled to cover up her ignited heart. "What is the path to it"

"Accepting yourself is the path. Surrender your mind to accepting yourself as it is, and accepting the world as it is. Once you have done it, everything that you do, will be in harmony with your inner self- or in other words, 'good deeds'. When you become true to yourself to the farthest end, a certain stage comes when you start enjoying your uniqueness. Spiritual plane of life is where you meet yourself without any veils"

Rinzen asks again "If some person acts rude or inappropriate to me, I become angry. So, accepting myself, I can continue becoming angry?"

Bankei (giggling): "You can show anger to ward off bad influences- there are people who can make your life difficult; people you need to avoid- it's a part of taking care of ourselves- that's a wise person's anger. He shows it; never becomes it. But when a fool gets angry, he becomes the anger. People being angry at unnecessary things- for example, if a person's ideology is different to you, and you engage in verbal battle to prove your point is right- or when you feel that you are not given the respect you deserve, or someone speaks very low of you, or a person who loved you, leaves you for no reason – likewise there are a lot of situations where people could avoid anger, but unfortunately they ignite it. Root of anger is the misunderstanding of your inner self. It is the reaction that you give when your egocentric delusions make you expect things to happen in a certain way, and it doesn't. A person who accepted the outer-world and inner-world as it is, will never get angry."

Rinzen's unhinged mind wiggled between light and dark. Bankei's words felt like concealed revelations to her. She continued questioning:

"Thinking logically, we all are animals living on this earth, just wanting to live a happy and comfortable life-there is no reason to be sad or angry"

"But, are you happy?"

"No".

Bankei: "Logic is a great thing. You can conduct your life in a better way if you apply rationalism. But life is mostly illogical. The existence of humans itself seems illogical to me"

Rinzen: "No, I have read in books- How life evolved from small organisms. I read the 'Ladder of life' by Aristotle, in which the organisms are classified into groups- which gave me an idea that all are linked to each other. In my view, human life must have evolved from small forms to complex forms, like us humans."

Bankei: "This world would exist in harmony without any human walking on it- humans are not at all needed for this earth. Haven't you seen serene forests? It is self-reliant with the flora and fauna. You living on this earth, is only a matter of yourself. The earth doesn't need you"

Rinzen: "Then what is the meaning of human life? why are we here and what are we supposed to do."

Bankei: "That's the toughest question ever asked. Haha"

Bankei effortlessly closed his eyes for a minute.

"When a flute aligns to the flow of air in a certain way, it creates music. If it doesn't it creates noise. Human aren't so different. When they align to their on inner self they become beutiful creatures. Every human has a copy of the whole universe inside- in the form of impressions; human is the consequence of a progression. As you said, the most advanced life form, progressively evolved right from the earliest organism. Evolving and improving in each step. That's the nature of our minds too- we constantly try ways to improve the experience of our existence in this world- that's the reason behind all the discoveries and inventions humans achieved."

"So, the purpose of life is to evolve?"

"Organisms evolved from one form to another as an expression of their will to survive. Why did they want to survive? Survival instinct is the one thing in common among all the animals, including us humans. Have you ever thought why this instinct is there?"

"Every animal wants to live, right? Every animal has the fear of death"

"The earth is made of rock and soil and water-at least as how it looks from the outside- it is lifeless matter. Earth doesn't want any organism to live, because it can remain as a sphere of soil, without any flora or fauna on it. Years and years ago, somehow, life started on earth, and it slowly progressed, evolved, and we all are here-think of the first life on earth- why did it try to survive and reproduce? Wasn't it its own independent will?"

"What's behind that will?"

"It's the art of knowing the universe. Every animal, wanted to know more-they wanted to explore; the strong desire to know the world- that reflects as survival instinct-or the wanting to live. The universe itself is contained in life- like water flows out of a pot when a hole is made in it, the universe which manifests as consciousness inside an organism, flows out through its senses, which is experienced by the organism as its mind. This flow of consciousness constantly occurs, from life till death- the mind is awake from birth till death; it constantly searches knowledge as experiences- to harmonize with the consciousness inside; or the universe inside. It requires highest level of experiences- first they knew the ocean- then they came to know the land- then they conquered the skies- when one form was not enough, they evolved- whatever they learnt was stored as memories and passed on to the next generation as traits and skills- and finally, life attained human form; the most advanced form of life- where the gap between inner consciousness and outer universe is the least; every human is only a line away from the highest experience of universe. Even though an advanced biological form, the mind of human is unfortunately as complicated as their systems are. Consciousness flows out through all 5 senses, reflecting the impressions in their minds- but the minds being so complicated, it always gives them a diminished experience."

"Why do people run behind material benefits then"

"No pleasure is material pleasure. All pleasures are connected to the soul. A drunkard drinks not for his body; but for the different experience of the world, he would get for a short period of time. That's why humans are so addicted to intoxicants- they are an easy ticket to a wider experience- but a pseudo one."

"An artist continues to make art, because his consciousness has found a channel to flow- it's his artistic skill. His mind is tuned that way, that it lets his consciousness flow out only through art- that's why artists are unable to take up any other profession, even if they go starving. Singers cannot do anything other than singing- a singer has to sing- that's the expression of their life force- and if they cannot find a living from that profession, they are in vain. You might have seen a lot of such artists. People running behind their passions even if it doesn't give them bread, is solely due to their strong innate instinct to understand the universe- to accomplish completeness."

"What spiritual practices does to you is that, it will help you tune your mind to conduct your inner consciousness in the easiest way. It will take away all the blockages in your mind, straighten it, thin it, and will make you aligned to the flow of consciousness from your own inside. Then, in every step, you will experience the whole universe- that's the state of enlightenment."

Bankei bowed to Rinzen, and left.

Circle

On a morning, at the garden-Bankei was watering the plants. Rinzen, on her morning walk, came near the Master.

"How are you, Rin?" Bankei asked.

"Today is the last day of submitting answers" A hopeless Rin said.

Rinzen had almost given up participating the contest, and her mind had started of thinking about other aspects. There was no reason for it, but the morning felt warm and joyful to her, flowers around her seemed pleasant and vibrant, mountains looked shiny, and she had an unhindered smile on her face.

"Meditate, until you find the key" Master Bankei said.

"At first, I thought those who have access to ancient geometry books could answer. But now it seems that too isn't working"

"When are you planning to leave to Xi Jian?"

"In a couple of days, Master"

Rinzen continued "Master! Why is this simple geometric shape so mysterious!! I happened to know that so many people sent answers regarding the inscribed angle, chords, and a lot of other geometrical properties. All of those answers got rejected. None of the answers satisfied their question, since all those were mere prewritten theories, they said"

"What was the question again? "

"Four figures are given- Circle, triangle, square and rectangle. Out of these, we have to point out the most special thing about circular shape"

Master Bankei divulged: "Knowledge and intellect is one thing; competition is another thing. In a competition, in order to find the correct answer, you have to understand the question as well as the questioner!"

Rinzen was perplexed.

"Here the questioner is the King. And you said none of the answers so far satisfied him. Indeed you got to understand from it, what would be the answer they are expecting"

Rinzen: "For a mathematical question, they must expect a mathematical answer, right? "

Bankei: "Need not be. All ancient mathematicians were philosophers too. Our king is known for his love of philosophical ideologies"

Rinzen thought deeply, for a moment.

"Yes. He has a dedicated council of professors to conduct philosophical debates"

"An endless circle creating endless problems" Rinzen commented.

"Well, you came very near to the answer, I sense that !!"

Rinzen: “What, master?”

“You just said the answer right now”

Rinzen: “An ‘endless circle creating’ Is that it? I suppose not, because that is the most obvious thing about a circle, that it has no ends unlike a square or triangle, and that answer was rejected at the beginning itself. It’s simply pointless, Master”

Bankei: “See? truth cannot be concealed long. Just now too, you said the answer”

Rinzen: “Please explain, master”

Bankei closed his eyes. He raised his forehead and showed his bald head towards the sky. After a few minutes he started to speak.

“You stand on how many legs?”

Rinzen: “Two”

A centipede stands on how many legs?

Rinzen: “A hundred”

Now tell me, “How does a square stand on the ground”

“With one side resting on the ground, master”

“How can you make a triangle rest on the ground?”

“One of the three sides resting on the ground”

Master’s words pierced like an arrow into her inner intellect, awakening her dormant geniuses. “How does a circle rest on the ground?” Bankei asked.

Rinzen’s intellect awoke. “On a single point”

Bankei stood up, came near, raised both hands and blessed his apprentice on her head. "This is the last and final discourse you will hear from me, my dear kid. Listen. A square, when its body gets bigger, takes bigger area to stand on the ground. So is rectangle, so is a triangle. They can grow big only if their base on ground is proportionally big, otherwise they would fall. But a circle, no matter how big it gets, even if it is of the size of the moon, it can stand on the ground, resting on merely a single point; a simple dot; having zero area. Be like a circle. No matter how great you become, the space you take from this earth be the least."

"You don't need any more teaching. I see your aura becoming wider and wider. I am giving you a koan. Start meditating on it. You will find the answer to it, and when that happens, you will be enlightened."

"Tell me master"

"Find the area of the point on which a sphere rests on a plain surface"

Master bowed and left.

Rinzen went in zazen. At the end of 41 days, she heard the soundless sound. She saw the shapeless shape- arealess area- the indivisible part of whole of existence- the single point from the whole existence came out from. Rinzen became the simplest person on earth.

A Year Later

It was the memorial-day of ancestors. King had arranged a big feast at his dinery. He had invited all his ministers, philosophers and poets. At the far end of that long table, the King majestically sat on his Golden throne. On the next seat to his right sat Rinzen. The King asked Rinzen:

"Respected Chief philosopher of my court- 'Shifu Rinzen', enlighten me. I want to know about the real essence of life. Can you teach me Zen?"

Rinzen, who was at that time tasting the soup, said: "There is too much lemon in this soup. Let us correct it first, then we shall learn Zen."